HEDGEHOGS

Don't Live in the City!

Written by Lucy Reynolds

Illustrated by Jenna Herman

Dusty houses, sooty eaves,
rustling piles of fallen leaves,

great tall windows, bright red doors,
a noisy bus that beeps and roars.

On and on the city goes, bustling busily by,

until…

A whistle and a purr make Grace stop
in her tracks.

Every time the leaves stir:
'Listen - what was that?'

But Archie shrugs and scoots on by.
'It must have been a cat.'

Whipping wind and stirring breeze
blasting bare the autumn trees.

Piles of amber, gold and red
gather on the road instead.

Down and down the foliage spins,
chestnut, oak and ash.

Until...

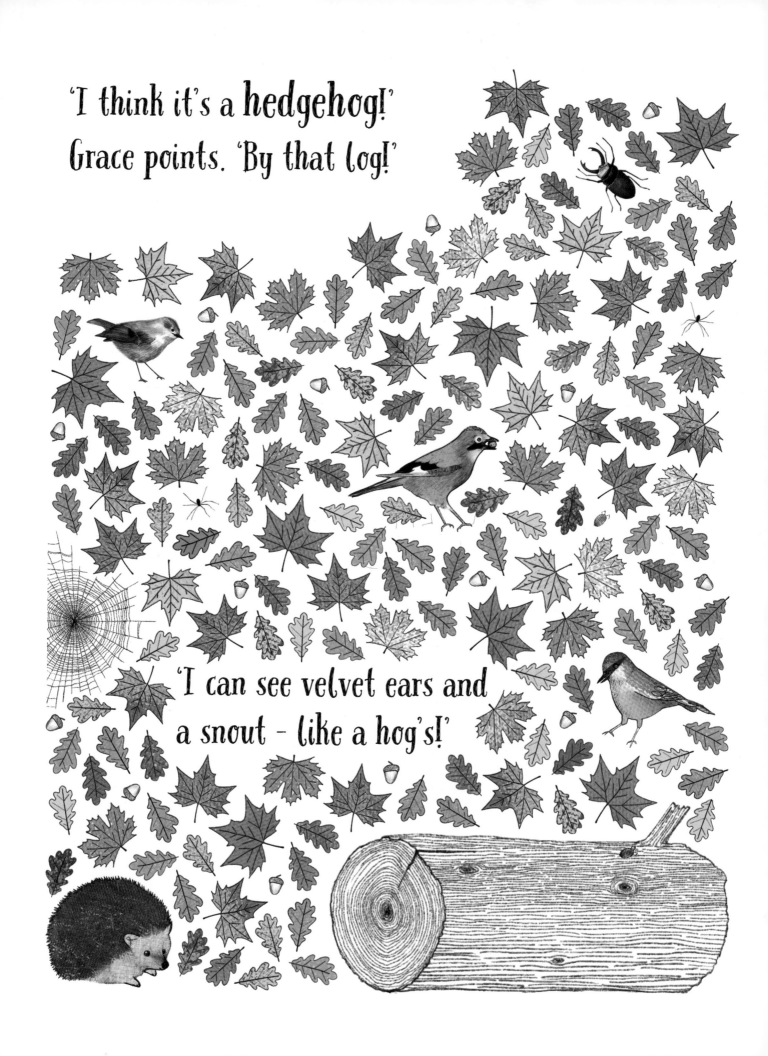

'I think it's a **hedgehog!**'
Grace points. 'By that log!'

'I can see velvet ears and
a snout – like a hog's!'

But Archie snorts
and rushes on.

'I bet it was a dog.'

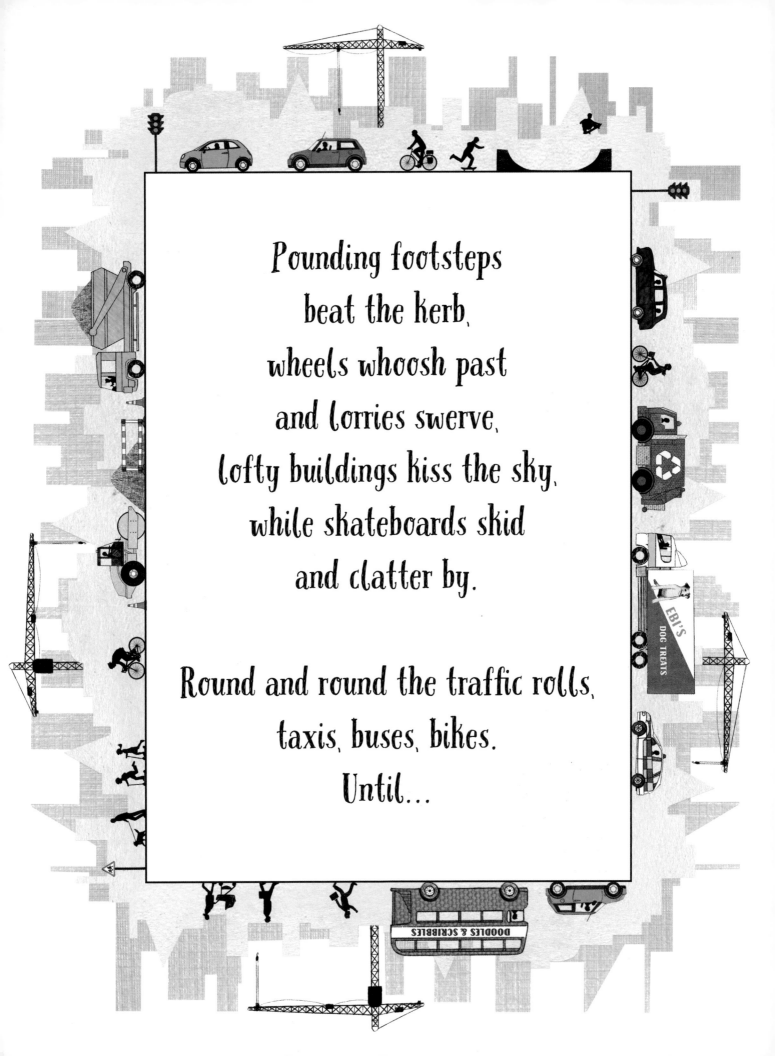

Pounding footsteps
beat the kerb,
wheels whoosh past
and lorries swerve,
lofty buildings kiss the sky,
while skateboards skid
and clatter by.

Round and round the traffic rolls,
taxis, buses, bikes.
Until...

'I'm *sure* it's a hedgehog!'
cries Grace in surprise,

as something small and prickly runs fast before her eyes.

But Archie shakes his head and shouts: 'A RAT!' Then off he flies.

Shrugging shoulders, knitted brow,
Grace gives up and thinks somehow
the thing she saw beside the road
must have been a mouse or toad.

Purrrrrrrrr

Up and up, they climb the hill,

as dusk begins to fall.

Then...

'Hedgehogs don't live in the city!'
Archie says to Grace.

'They live in the countryside
– a green and peaceful place.'

cock-a-doodle-do

honk honk

twit-twoo

squeak squeak

'They're very rare and hard to spot,
— so difficult to trace.'

GO

But by the crossing *something's* there –
with stumpy tail and spiky hair.

Secretly it darts along
through the surging city throng.

On and on it weaves its way,
tiny, spiny, round.
Until…

High Street
Love Street
The School
The Shops

It stops and softly sniffs the air
- where's it travelling to?

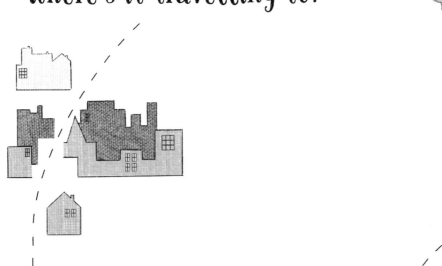

Pootling past a post box,
to a gate, then through,

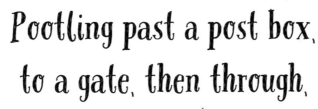

scampering by the lit-up
shops and round a bin or two.

Sudden whoosh - a windy gust
lifts the piles of twigs and dust.

Blowing high, they dance and spin -

but what's this they're uncovering?

One by one the leaves reveal
the most amazing sight.
It is...

A hedgehog with her babies,
curled up in a nest,

with jet-black eyes and soft, pink paws –
tucked tight against their chests.

purrrrrrrrrr

And, as they gently purr, their
tummies lift then come to rest.

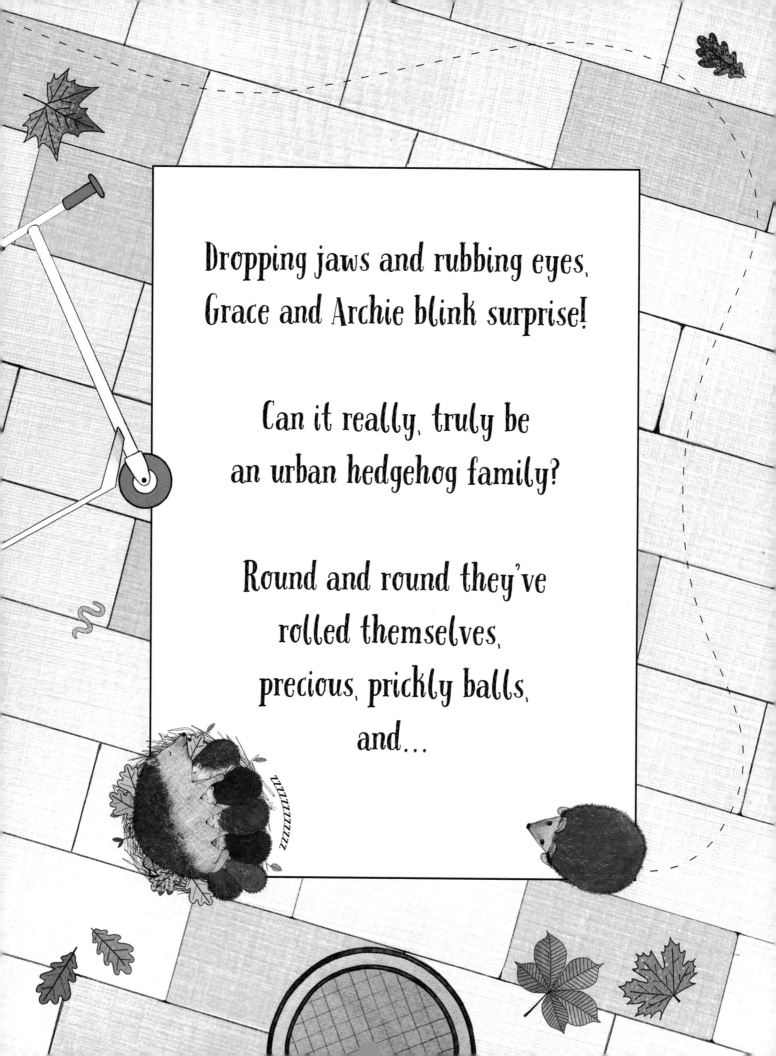

Dropping jaws and rubbing eyes,
Grace and Archie blink surprise!

Can it really, truly be
an urban hedgehog family?

Round and round they've
rolled themselves,
precious, prickly balls,
and…

'It WAS a little hedgehog!'
Grace cries out in amazement,
as she spots *our* little hedgehog
join the nest beside the pavement
and his furzy family sleeping in
their leafy, warm encasement.

One last puff – the wind drops,
twirling twigs slow and stop.
Blanket-like they hide again
the hedgehogs in their secret den.

On and on

the leaves drift down,

covering them from view.

So...

If one day you think *you've*
seen a little creature creep

beneath a pile of fallen leaves,
be sure to pause and peep.

in case *you* glimpse a wondrous
ball, curled up fast asleep.

THE END

HOGGY

The word 'hedgehog' comes
from a combination of two words:
'hedge' (where they live)
plus 'hog' (from their pig-like snouts).

An average adult hedgehog has about
6,000 spines on its back! What do you
think a hedgehog's spine might feel like?

If they feel threatened, hedgehogs can
curl into a tight ball and stay still.

A group of hedgehogs is called
an 'array' or a 'prickle'!

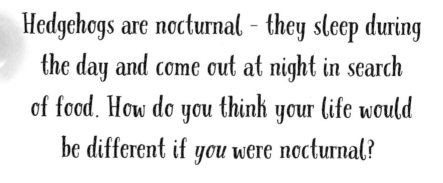

Hedgehogs are nocturnal - they sleep during
the day and come out at night in search
of food. How do you think your life would
be different if *you* were nocturnal?

FACTS

Hedgehogs are insect-eaters,
and enjoy snuffling about for slugs, snails,
beetles, worms and other creepy-crawlies.
Can you forage for a hedgehog's supper
hidden within the pages of our book?

A baby hedgehog is called a 'hoglet'.
Mothers usually give birth to a litter of
four to six young in the spring, and sometimes
have a second litter in the autumn.

Hedgehogs hibernate through the winter
in a snug nest of grass and leaves.

You can tell how a hedgehog is feeling from
the noises he makes: whistling and purring
mean he is happy! Snorting, puffing, clicking or
hissing mean he is not. What other animal purrs when
when it's happy and hisses when it isn't?

HELP OUR HEDGEHOGS!

Hedgehogs are a species in decline and could soon become extinct. Although we think hedgehogs mainly live in the countryside, their numbers are falling fastest in rural areas. This is because intensive farming has removed many of their hedgerow nesting sites and reduced the number of slugs and grubs available for them to eat.

Luckily, hedgehogs have adapted well to urban living and are disappearing less quickly in towns and cities. Urban hedgehogs seek out green spaces such as parks, cemeteries, wasteland, railway banks and gardens.

Wherever you live, here are some ways that you can help our precious hedgehogs:

 Join gardens together by making little holes in neighbouring fences so that hedgehogs can roam and forage freely

 Leave wild areas and log piles to attract tasty insects

Avoid using slug pellets and pesticides – they are poisonous to hedgehogs and remove a vital food source

 Create a hedgehog house and feeding station in a green space near you (stocked with meaty cat or dog food and water – never milk!)

 Check for sleeping hedgehogs before anybody mows the lawn or starts a bonfire

 If you find a hedgehog you're concerned about, ask a grown up to gently pick it up wearing gardening gloves. Bring it inside and put it in a high-sided cardboard box with an old towel or fleece in the bottom for the hedgehog to hide under.

As long as the hedgehog isn't bleeding, place a hot water bottle wrapped in a towel in the box, so that it has a gentle heat source (make sure the bottle doesn't go cold), and put the box somewhere quiet and safe. Offer meaty cat or dog food and fresh water, then phone your nearest hedgehog charity or animal sanctuary as soon as possible for help and advice.

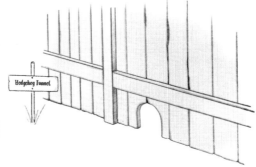

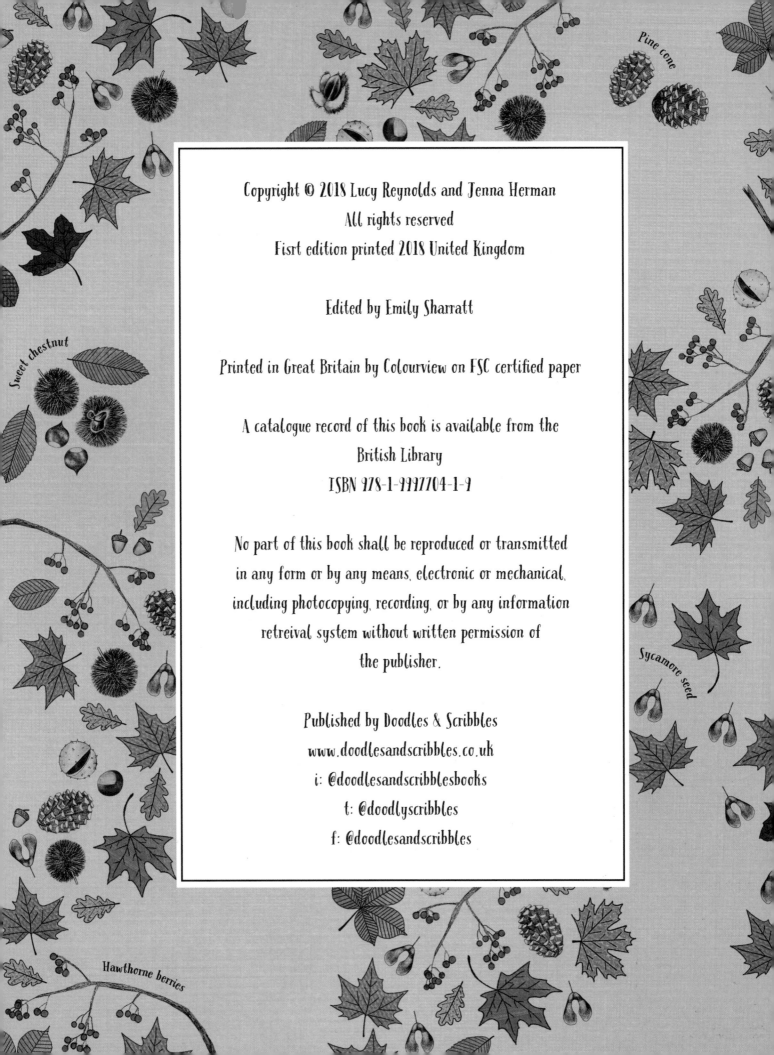

Edited by Emily Sharratt

Printed in Great Britain by Colourview on FSC certified paper

A catalogue record of this book is available from the
British Library
ISBN 978-1-9997704-1-9

Published by Doodles & Scribbles
www.doodlesandscribbles.co.uk
i: @doodlesandscribblesbooks
t: @doodlyscribbles
f: @doodlesandscribbles